Thoughts and Dreams: A Collection of Poems

Davion Moore

BookLeaf Publishing

India | USA | UK

Presentation by *BookLeaf Publishing*

Web: www.bookleafpub.com

E-mail: info@bookleafpub.com

ISBN : 9789357448451

First edition 2021

Wishes

Wishes are dreams
 Yet to come true
Desires that have yet to manifest

We hold them near and dear
To our hearts
Cherish them

Home

A home can be a sanctuary,
At a moment
Where things get out of hand.
Once you get into it,
Enjoy it.
Remember old,fond memories
Tucked in your mind like
A hidden treasure.
As the home holds all
Past, present, and future.

Exploration

Pursuing opportunities
That scare me.
Like a child,
Being scared of the dark.

Unsure of what's next.
So much uncertainty.
But what's worse
Than doing something?
Doing nothing.

So I guess I'll just be scared.

Unconditional Love

There's nothing like
The love of a family
Lifting you up,
When you're at your lowest.
Recharging you,
When your battery's dying.
Making you laugh,
In your most painful moments.
Just being there
When it's needed.

A love so precious
So pure, so genuine
Like a bird's first flight,
Soaring to new heights.

A blessing and a gift,
This love so true.
And it warms one's heart to hear
I love you.

Starchaser

It seems like an eternity ago
A time when the star I wished on
Flew through the sky
And I have yet to see another
So radiant

Opportunities

Opportunities come up
At the strangest times
But at the best times

"Social Media"

On Tuesday
A discussion on social media
Was brought up to friends
Who thought that
Other people's lives
Seem much more exciting
Hint: they're not

Seeking(A Blackout Poem)

The more we look,
The more we find
Mystifying and wonderful
Brilliant
Examine life,
And Death
Sites
Significant symbols
Sacred
Behold marvelous
Existence
Cherish the site
That still exists
Positioned in elaborate stances
Soar in the afterlife
And heal

Hidden Treasures

The world's cities have stories to tell
Written down in the most unlikely places
Abandoned buildings
Desolate subway stations
The hidden treasures of the chest
That is the city
The heartbeat that gives life
To a place that never sleeps
Take me away to the places I seek

No Comment (A Blackout)

Ask them
They have all the answers

History

Photos of the past present
Things unfamiliar
To the present
To see a person
Feel their presence
Feel their emotion
Connect with them
Think their thoughts
And as you look into this antique mirror
You see history

The Night Owl

The night owl searches
The bright night sky for answers
To life's hard questions

Intention

The day after
The star spoke
About intention
I chose to listen

The Trap

The darkness, the wicked
Moves like a black smog
In a polluted area.
Selfishness,
Manipulation,
Wrap their hands around
One's neck.
Cutting off
The ability to breathe.
Calling for help,
In a still,windowless room.
Like a tree in falling in the forest,
Am I even being heard?
Or are my calls falling upon deaf ears?
But I cannot give up.
Must continue.
On and on and on.
Help me, please.
Let me out before it's too late.

Soar

The moment the sky
Made their hardest days lighter
They soared

Caged Bird

Some day
You will be
Released

Seasons Change

Time is seasons
Springing into action
Falling like a leaf
Onto the colorful ground
Season change
But the memories don't
So let's cherish them forever

The Emcee

The emcee took the stage
The mic tightly gripped
A swagger to his walk
A bounce in his shoulders
An attitude like a young bull
Confidence that could rival Ali.
He captivates the crowd,
As his words paint a picture,
Of a world foreign to them.
The lyrics flow gently from his lips,
Like a babbling brook.
Captivating the audience,
And leaving them shook.
The emcee speaks,
And the audience listens.
To his deepest thoughts,
And complex visions.
Rock the crowd emcee,
Rock the crowd.
With that fresh hip hop sound.

Sister Moon

Night falls and the world is silent
Hours are irrelevant, hours are timeless.
The sun doesn't shine.
It remains shy,
And reluctant to show itself
So its sister takes it place.
Sister moon is out
Sister moon is out
Look up y'all sister moon is out.

Untitled

Removing negativity
From one's life
Can free you in ways
You cannot imagine

The Weight of the World

The weight of the world,
Is a burden on my back
While try to maintain,
And keep my soul intact

Perhaps these weights
Are illusions, farces
Who's purpose is to trap
This reclusive artist

It's getting heavier and heavier,
Scarier and deadlier
A weight so profound,
Trying to hold you down

The weight of the world
Is a burden on my back
While trying to maintain
And keep my soul intact